NOT-SO-ORDINARY SCIENCE

GET NOISY WITH SCIENCE!

PROJECTS WITH SOUNDS, MUSIC, AND MORE

by Elsie Olson

CAPSTONE PRESS
a capstone imprint

Dabble Lab is published by Capstone Press, an imprint of Capstone.
1710 Roe Crest Drive, North Mankato, Minnesota 56003
capstonepub.com

Copyright © 2023 by Capstone. All rights reserved. No part of this publication may be reproduced in whole or in part, or stored in a retrieval system, or transmitted in any form or by any means, electronic, mechanical, photocopying, recording, or otherwise, without written permission of the publisher.

Library of Congress Cataloging-in-Publication Data is available on the Library of Congress website.
ISBN: 9781666342277 (hardcover)
ISBN: 9781666342284 (ebook PDF)

Summary: Do you like to get noisy? These science projects are for you! Craft a pan flute out of drinking straws. Make a spooky wailing balloon. Then, learn the science behind each nifty noise!

Image Credits
Shutterstock: Blan-k (music notes), Front Cover, 31, ONYXprj (background), Front Cover, Back Cover, Valenty (sound wave), Front Cover, 28, Zerbor (bells), Front Cover, 8, Bohdan Populov (radar waves), 3, 14, alarich, 4 (string), arsslawa, 4, 26 (rubber bands), Love the wind, 4 (glitter), Natakorn Ruangrit (scissors), 4, 10, Passakorn sakulphan, 4 (straws), Sergei Bogachov (glue gun), 4, 30, titov dmitriy, 4 (paper cup), wk1003mike (balloons), 4, 26, Scarabea (cups connected by string), 5, 12, SweetLemons, 6 (googly eyes), Marxstudio, 10 (tape), Picsfive, 12 (string), P-Square Studio, 12 (paper cup), Na be lazy, 14 (marbles and dice), PaulPaladin (hex nuts), 14, 15, Elizabeth A.Cummings, 16 (food coloring), marla dawn studio (metal spoon), 16, 17, Anastasia_Panait, 20 (feathers), paranut, 22 (paper roll), Svitlana Martynova, 22 (paint and paintbrushes), arslaan, 24 (speaker), Igartist 79, 24 (eggs), Vitaly Zorkin, 26 (pencil), Ekaterina43, 28 (hook-and-loop tape), 30 (bobby pins)

Design Elements
Shutterstock: MicroOne (gauges)
All project photos shot by Mighty Media, Inc.

Editorial Credits
Editor: Jessica Rusick
Designer: Aruna Rangarajan

All internet sites appearing in back matter were available and accurate when this book was sent to press.

The publisher and the author shall not be liable for any damages allegedly arising from the information in this book, and they specifically disclaim any liability from the use or application of any of the contents of this book.

Printed and bound in the USA. PO4882

TABLE OF CONTENTS

Make Some Noise! 4

Dancing Glitter 6

Underwater Bell 8

Fancy Flute 10

Not-So-Mobile Phone 12

Wailing Balloon. 14

Stellar Xylophone. 16

Flying Buzzer. 18

Screeching Owl 20

Box & Band Guitar. 22

Soundproof Headphones 24

Different Drums 26

Doppler Catch 28

Petite Piano. 30

Read More 32

Internet Sites 32

MAKE SOME NOISE!

What happens when experiments screech and gadgets buzz? It turns out super-loud science projects also happen to be fantastically fun. So grab your earplugs, put on your lab coat, and turn up the volume.

THINGS ARE ABOUT TO GET NOISY!

GENERAL SUPPLIES & TOOLS

balloons

drinking straws

duct tape

glitter

hot glue gun

paper cups

pushpins

rubber bands

scissors

string

· · · · TIPS & TRICKS · · · ·

FOLLOW THESE SIMPLE TIPS TO STAY SAFE AND HAVE FUN!

◆ **Read all the steps** and gather all your supplies before starting a project.

◆ **These projects are noisy!** Be considerate and do these projects during the day. Make sure those around you don't mind a little noise!

◆ **Ask an adult** to help when using hot or sharp tools.

· · · · SCIENCE TERMS TO KNOW · · · ·

CENTRIPETAL FORCE (sen-TRI-puh-tuhl FORS): the force that keeps an object revolving around a center point moving in a circular path

FREQUENCY (FREE-kwuhn-see): how often a sound wave repeats over a period of time. Sound waves with a high frequency produce high-pitched sounds.

FRICTION (FRIK-shuhn): the force that slows down objects when they come into contact with one another

PITCH (PICH): how high or low a musical note sounds

WAVELENGTH (WAYV-length): the distance between two high points in a sound wave. Sound waves with long wavelengths produce low-pitched sounds.

DANCING GLITTER

Make some glitter hop and groove when you **sing into a cardboard tube!**

WHAT YOU NEED

- paper towel tube
- scissors
- pencil
- plastic or cardboard container
- duct tape
- balloon
- craft knife
- art supplies, such as glue, googly eyes & construction paper
- glitter

EXPERIMENT! TRY SINGING AT DIFFERENT PITCHES AND VOLUMES. WHAT HAPPENS?

WHAT YOU DO

STEP 1
Cut a paper towel tube in half horizontally on a diagonal. Tape the halves back together at an angle.

STEP 2
Trace one end of the tube onto the plastic or cardboard container. Cut out the hole using a craft knife.

STEP 3
Poke one end of the angled tube through the hole and tape it in place to secure.

STEP 4
Cut the tip off the balloon and stretch it over the container's opening. Decorate the container!

STEP 5
Pour glitter on top of the balloon. Sing into the tube and watch the glitter dance and bounce!

WHAT YOU GET

Membrane motion. The balloon stretched across the container is a membrane. As you sing into the tube, the vibrations from your voice cause air inside the container to vibrate the membrane. This causes the glitter to bounce around. **That's science!**

7

UNDERWATER BELL

A whale's song can be heard from thousands of miles away. How does sound travel so well underwater? Make a **waterproof bell** to find out!

WHAT YOU NEED

- clean tin can
- art supplies
- hammer & nail
- wire
- scissors
- ruler
- small bells
- tub or sink full of water

EXPERIMENT! TRY THIS AT A BEACH OR IN A POOL. DUNK YOUR HEAD AND RING THE BELL. WHAT DO YOU HEAR?

WHAT YOU DO

STEP 1
Decorate a tin can. Use a hammer and nail to poke a hole through the can's bottom.

STEP 2
Cut a length of wire 6 inches (15 centimeters) long and twist one end around the hangers of two small bells.

STEP 3
Poke the untwisted end of the wire into the tin can and up through the hole. Twist to secure. Ring the bell and listen to what it sounds like.

STEP 4
Now ring the bell underwater. How is the sound different?

WHAT YOU GET

A different kind of wave. Sound travels in waves. These waves are created by vibrations. Waves travel more quickly in dense substances, and faster waves make a noise seem louder. Water is denser than air. So, the bell sounds louder and clearer underwater. **That's science!**

9

FANCY FLUTE

A few straws, some cardboard, and a bit of tape are all you need to make **beautiful music!**

WHAT YOU NEED

- 4 drinking straws
- scissors
- cardboard
- ruler
- duct tape

WHAT YOU DO

STEP 1
Cut the straws so they are all slightly different lengths.

STEP 2
Cut two strips of cardboard about 1 inch (2.5 cm) wide and 6 inches (15 cm) long. Cut two pieces of duct tape slightly shorter than the cardboard.

STEP 3
Roll each piece of tape lengthwise with the sticky side out. Place each tape roll on a cardboard strip. Place the straws shortest to longest on one piece of tape, lining up the tops of the straws.

STEP 4
Place the second cardboard strip sticky side down on top of the straws so it lines up with the bottom strip.

STEP 5
Blow across the straw openings to make sound. How does the sound change as you blow across the different straw lengths?

WHAT YOU GET

Perfect pitch. When you blow air across a straw opening, the air vibrates inside the straw, making sound. The wavelength of the vibrations changes depending on the straw's length. This creates different pitches. **That's science!**

NOT-SO-MOBILE PHONE

Which type of string carries sound the best? Find out with this **cup-and-string sound experiment!**

WHAT YOU NEED

- 6 to 8 paper or plastic cups
- pushpin
- sharpened pencil
- scissors
- ruler
- different types of wire or string, such as yarn, thread & twine
- partner

EXPERIMENT!
WHAT HAPPENS WHEN YOU USE DIFFERENT LENGTHS OF STRING?

WHAT YOU DO

STEP 1
Use a pushpin to poke a hole in the bottoms of two cups. Use a sharpened pencil to widen the hole as needed.

STEP 2
Cut a length of string 8 to 10 feet (2 to 3 meters) long.

STEP 3
Poke each end of the string up through the bottom of a cup and knot inside the cup to secure.

Repeat **steps 1 through 3** using other types of string.

STEP 4
Give a partner one cup. Stand far away from each other so the string between the cups is stretched tight. Have your partner speak into their cup while you hold your cup to your ear.

STEP 5
Speak and listen with each cup and string set. How does the sound change?

WHAT YOU GET

Vibrations on the move. When you speak into the cup, your voice vibrates the air inside. These vibrations pass through the bottom of the cup, down the string, and into the other cup. Thin, tight strings carry sound better than thick, loose strings. **That's science!**

13

WAILING BALLOON

Is there a ghost in the lab? Roll a hex nut and other objects around inside a balloon for some **spooky sound effects!**

WHAT YOU NEED

- balloons
- hex nuts
- other small objects, such as pebbles, dice & marbles

EXPERIMENT! TRY BLOWING UP THE BALLOONS TO DIFFERENT SIZES. HOW DOES THE SOUND CHANGE?

WHAT YOU DO

STEP 1
Insert a hex nut through a balloon's neck. Blow up the balloon and tie the end.

STEP 2
Hold the tied end of the balloon in your palm. Rotate the balloon until the hex nut starts rolling around.

STEP 3
Keep rotating the balloon, building up speed until you start hearing a spooky noise. Then stop rotating the balloon. What happens?

STEP 4
Try this experiment again with other small objects. How does the sound change?

WHAT YOU GET

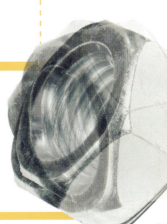

Forces and motion. As the six sides of the hex nut roll inside the balloon, they vibrate against the balloon wall, making a wailing sound. Centripetal force keeps the hex nut spinning even after you've stopped rotating the balloon. **That's science!**

15

STELLAR XYLOPHONE

Make some **beautiful music** while learning how water affects pitch!

WHAT YOU NEED

- 4 to 6 identical glass jars
- water
- food coloring
- art supplies, such as chenille stems, googly eyes & glue
- metal spoon

EXPERIMENT! BUILD A SIMILAR XYLOPHONE USING DIFFERENT LIQUIDS. TRY JUICE OR MILK!

16

WHAT YOU DO

STEP 1
Fill each jar with a different amount of water.

STEP 2
Add a different food coloring to each jar. If you'd like, decorate your jars to look like aliens or other creatures.

STEP 3
Lightly tap a metal spoon against the side of each jar. What do you notice?

WHAT YOU GET

Switching pitches. Tapping the spoon against the jars creates vibrations. Water slows down the movement of the vibrations. Slower vibrations make lower pitches. So, the glass with the most water will have the lowest pitch. **That's science!**

FLYING BUZZER

Make a nifty noisemaker that sounds just like a **buzzing swarm of insects!**

WHAT YOU NEED

- 2 index cards
- clear tape
- craft stick
- craft foam
- ruler
- scissors
- string
- wide rubber band

EXPERIMENT! CUT SMALL SLITS ALONG THE EDGES OF THE INDEX CARDS. WHAT HAPPENS?

18

WHAT YOU DO

STEP 1
Tape an index card to either side of a craft stick.

STEP 2
Cut two strips of craft foam, each 4 inches (10 cm) long and the width of the craft stick.

STEP 3
Fold one craft foam strip in half widthwise. Fold the strip again around the end of the craft stick and tape it in place. Repeat on the other side of the craft stick.

STEP 4
Cut a string 3 feet (0.9 m) long and tie it to one end of the craft stick, over the craft foam. Stretch a rubber band across the length of the craft stick and craft foam.

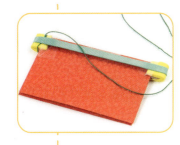

STEP 5
Use the string to spin the buzzer around in circles. What happens?

WHAT YOU GET

Vibration amplification. When you swing the noisemaker around, the air vibrates the rubber band, making a buzzing noise. The index cards amplify the sound, or make it louder. **That's science!**

19

SCREECHING OWL

Use the science of sound to turn a regular foam cup into a **screeching snowy owl pal!**

WHAT YOU NEED

- string
- scissors
- ruler
- sponge
- pushpin
- foam cup
- sharpened pencil
- paper clip
- art supplies, such as markers, glue & feathers
- water

EXPERIMENT! TRY USING DIFFERENT STRINGS. HOW DO THE SOUNDS CHANGE?

WHAT YOU DO

STEP 1
Cut a piece of string 12 inches (30.5 cm) long. Cut the sponge to make a piece about 1 to 2 inches (2.5 to 5 cm) wide.

STEP 2
Tie one end of the string around the sponge piece. Tie a small loop in the other end of the string.

STEP 3
Poke a hole through the bottom of the cup with a pushpin.

STEP 4
Use a sharpened pencil to widen the hole until it is large enough to insert the looped end of the string through. Attach a paper clip to the loop. Decorate the cup to look like an owl.

STEP 5
Wet the sponge and squeeze it around the string inside the cup. Pull down firmly and quickly. What happens?

WHAT YOU GET

Fun with friction. When you pull the wet sponge down the string, the friction from the sponge vibrates the string. The vibrations also travel through the air around the string. The cup's shape helps amplify the vibrations, making them louder. **That's science!**

BOX & BAND GUITAR

Let's make some music!
Use cardboard and rubber bands to make your own playable guitar.

WHAT YOU NEED

- shallow cardboard box with lid
- duct tape
- bowl
- pencil
- craft knife
- long, sturdy cardboard tube
- brass brads
- 4 to 6 rubber bands of various thicknesses
- pushpins
- art supplies

WHAT YOU DO

STEP 1
Tape the box lid closed if necessary. Place a bowl in the center of the box and trace around it. Cut out the circle.

STEP 2
Press one end of the cardboard tube against a short end of the box. Trace around the tube and cut out the circle.

STEP 3
Slide the cardboard tube a few inches into the hole. Use brads or duct tape to secure it.

STEP 4
Cut the rubber bands. Poke small holes near the top of the cardboard tube. Thread one end of each rubber band through the holes and knot to secure. Stretch the rubber bands beneath the large hole and use pushpins to secure them. This makes guitar strings.

STEP 5
Tape the ends of the rubber bands to secure. Decorate your guitar. Then pluck the strings!

WHAT YOU GET

Shimmying strings. When you pluck a rubber band, it vibrates. Energy from the vibrations travels across the box and into the hollow body, which amplifies the sound. Thicker rubber bands vibrate more slowly, making lower pitches.
That's science!

SOUNDPROOF HEADPHONES

Sometimes we need **peace and quiet!** Make your own soundproof headphones with everyday materials.

WHAT YOU NEED

- paper towel tube
- scissors
- ruler
- yarn
- hot glue gun
- 2 fillable plastic eggs
- pencil
- cardboard
- headband
- radio, speaker, or other music player
- cotton balls

EXPERIMENT! TRY OTHER SOUNDPROOFING MATERIALS, SUCH AS BUBBLE WRAP, FOAM, FABRIC, AND MORE!

24

WHAT YOU DO

STEP 1
Cut two rings about 1 inch (2.5 cm) wide out of a paper towel tube. Wrap each ring in yarn, gluing in place as needed.

STEP 2
Trace an egg top two times on cardboard to make two circles. Cut them out.

STEP 3
Wrap the headband and cardboard circles in yarn, gluing in place as needed.

STEP 4
Glue the rings to the rims of two egg tops. Glue each egg top to one end of the headband, making headphones.

STEP 5
Turn on music. Put on your headphones. What do you hear? Next, try filling the headphones with cotton balls. Push the yarn-covered circles into the rings to cover the cotton balls. What do you hear now?

Sound stoppers. Sound travels easily through some materials, like water and air. Other materials, like cotton and yarn, absorb sound vibrations. They can be used to block sound. **That's science!**

25

DIFFERENT DRUMS

Get ready to march to the beat of your own drum! This fun sound experiment is the perfect way to **play with pitch!**

WHAT YOU NEED

- balloons
- scissors
- 3 to 4 containers of different sizes
- rubber bands
- art supplies
- 2 pencils with erasers

26

WHAT YOU DO

STEP 1
Cut the neck off a balloon. Stretch the balloon over the opening of a container to make a drum.

STEP 2
Wrap a rubber band around the container to secure the balloon.

Repeat **steps 1 and 2** for each container.

STEP 3
Decorate your drum set!

STEP 4
Use the eraser end of pencils to beat the drums. How does the sound change between drums?

WHAT YOU GET

The power of pitch. Because your containers are different sizes, some balloons are stretched tighter than others. The tightness of a drum's skin affects its pitch. The tighter the skin, the higher the pitch. Loose skin makes a lower pitch. **That's science!**

DOPPLER CATCH

Find a pal and play a noisy game of catch to learn about **physics at work!**

WHAT YOU NEED

- plastic ball
- craft knife
- duct tape
- hook-and-loop tape
- ruler
- small battery-powered buzzer or other noisemaker
- partner

28

WHAT YOU DO

STEP 1
Cut the ball in half. Match the two halves back together. Place a small strip of duct tape between them to make a hinge.

STEP 2
Use duct tape to cover the rough edges of each half of the ball.

STEP 3
Attach three small strips of hook-and-loop tape next to the ball's opening, opposite the hinge.

STEP 4
Fold three 3-inch (8 cm) pieces of duct tape in half lengthwise, sticky sides in. Stick a piece of hook-and-loop tape to one end of each strip. Tape the other ends of the strips to the side of the ball without hook-and-loop tape. Attach the hook-and-loop tape pieces together to make flaps.

STEP 5
Cover the rest of the ball in duct tape. Turn on the buzzer and put it in the ball. Close the flaps. Toss the ball back and forth to a partner. How does the sound change?

WHAT YOU GET

The Doppler effect. As a source of sound gets closer to a listener, the frequency of the sound waves increases. This means the sound's pitch gets higher. As the source moves away, the pitch gets lower. This is known as the Doppler effect. **That's science!**

PETITE PIANO

Explore sound waves and pitch by making a **pocket-sized piano.** This itty-bitty instrument packs a punch!

WHAT YOU NEED

- small, sturdy cardboard box with a lid
- tape
- scissors
- 2 craft sticks
- hot glue gun
- 5 bobby pins

WHAT YOU DO

STEP 1
Tape the box lid closed if necessary. Cut a hole in the top of the box.

STEP 2
Trim two craft sticks to the box's width. Glue one craft stick to the box above the hole.

STEP 3
Pry the bobby pins apart at different angles. Arrange them on the craft stick in order of angle size.

STEP 4
Tape the straight ends of the bobby pins to the craft stick so the pins hang over the hole. Glue the other craft stick on top of the bobby pins so it lines up with the first craft stick.

STEP 5
Flick the top of each bobby pin downward quickly. What do you hear?

WHAT YOU GET

All about angles. When you flick the bobby pin, it vibrates the air around it. The box amplifies the sound. The bobby pins at smaller angles create faster vibrations when flicked. This produces higher pitches. **That's science!**

READ MORE

Claybourne, Anna. *Recreate Discoveries about Sound*. New York: Crabtree Publishing, 2019.

Felix, Rebecca. *Crayola Super Simple STEAM Activities*. Minneapolis: Lerner Publications, 2022.

Sohn, Emily. *Adventures in Sound with Max Axiom Super Scientist: An Augmented Reading Science Experience*. North Mankato, MN: Capstone Press, 2019.

INTERNET SITES

DK Find Out!—Sound
dkfindout.com/us/science/sound

Science Buddies—Experiment with Acoustics Science Projects
sciencebuddies.org/science-fair-projects/project-ideas/experiment-with-acoustics

Science Kids—The Science of Sound for Kids
sciencekids.co.nz/sound.html